Detroit Latin Sounds in Poetry

La Onda Latina en Poesia-Detroit

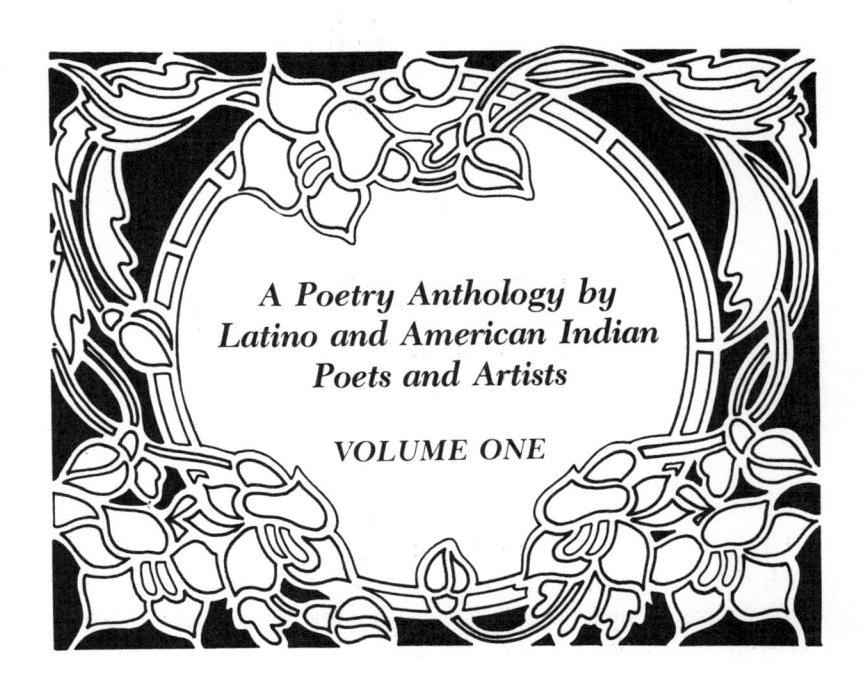

A Poetry Anthology by
Latino and American Indian
Poets and Artists

VOLUME ONE

Published by
CASA DE UNIDAD

Michigan Council
for the Arts

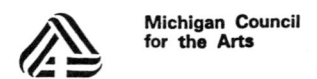

National
Endowment
for the Arts

Copyright © 1985
Casa de Unidad
1920 Scotten
Detroit, Michigan 48209

All rights reserved. Copyright for individual poems remains with the poet. Copyright for artwork remains with the artist. This book, or parts thereof, may not be reproduced without written permission of Casa de Unidad.

International Standard Book No. 0-9615977-0-4

Library of Congress Catalog Card No. 85-73152

Acknowledgements

A *special thanks to:*
Michigan Council for the Arts
Casa De Unidad
José L. Garza, project coordinator
Karen Gatrell
Litho/Color, Inc., typesetting
David Conklin, printer

Table of Contents

Anibal Bourdon............................ 1
Ruby M. Burns............................. 6
Ana Cardona............................... 7
Marcelle Douglas..........................15
José L. Garza.............................16
Hernán Castellano-Giroń...................19
Marycruz Soto Gonzalez....................22
Victoria González.........................23
Lolita Hernandez-Gray.....................25
William Augustus Hollier..................29
Fred Mora.................................31
William Mora, Jr..........................33
Delfin Muñoz..............................36
Rosa Maria Muñoz..........................41
Nemene....................................45
Patti Orozco..............................49
Rachel Perazza............................54
Abel Piñeiro..............................55
Carolina Ramon............................57
Marc Sanchez..............................59
Jacqueline Sanchez........................62
Trinidad Sánchez, S.J., Hno...............65

The artists are Ana Luisa Barreto, Anibal Bourdon, Ana Cardona, Lana Douglas, José L. Garza, Hernán Castellano-Girón, Warren Augustus Hollier, William Mora, Jr., and Julio Perazza

COVER DESIGN BY PATTI OROZCO.

"Love is the key; it is the force that propels us toward writing/painting/acting. To see squalor and not protest is to deny our humanity. To act with people toward nation building is to affirm our human-ness and to show love for our progeny and all humanity."

RICARDO SANCHEZ, Poet
–text taken from his book entitled:
HECHIZOSPELLS.

LA ONDA LATINA EN POESIA-DETROIT is a celebration—a celebration of discovery of poets and artists from our community in Southwest Detroit. This anthology is a celebration of the culture that oftentimes lies hidden away in the drawers of desks/bureaus and notebooks in silence and unseen.

It is a celebration of 'Latino Sounds'—that is, 'sounds by Latinos' (Mexican, Puerto Rican, Chicano, Central American and Native American people) and in some instances it is about Latinos. It is a new celebration, in a way, for it is the first effort by CASA DE UNIDAD and some artists and poets in the community to come together—sharing art and poems—sharing sounds for nation building.

It is a celebration that we hope will continue to encourage, to challenge others in this community to be proud of their culture and not be afraid or reticent in sharing their talents. In a city torn by unemployment, drugs, high crime rates, gentrification and all other urban ills—Raza 'celebrates life' in her art and poems.

It is a celebration that gives hope and that drives us to write/paint/and act for a better society—where there is justice for all.

*Respectfully,
for The Editorial Committee,
Trinidad Sánchez, S.J., Hno.*

Anibal Bourdon

Mi Tierra Natal

Hay tantas cosas bonitas,
En mi terruño natal,
Hay hileras de palmeras,
Y rosas en mi rosal.

Hay playas que son encantos,
Bellas las olas del mar
Flores en los cafetales,
Y aromas a naranjar.

Cuando la caña florece,
La brisa su pelo peina
Y en sus ojas ya resecas,
Hace su nido la reina.

Al llegar el nuevo dia
Canta alegre el Ruiseñor,
Y se ven las mariposas,
Volando de flor en flor.

Y cuando llega la zafra,
Canta alegre el campesino
Por que de ella saca el Rom
Y suda para sus hijos.

Anibal Bourdon

Tu Nieto Mayor

Toma esta flor Abuelita,
Que Papito te mandó
Es a nombre de Mamita
De mis Hermanos y yo.

Tambien un beso bien grande,
De mi parte te daré
Llevalo siempre en tu pecho
Que yo no te olvidaré.

Yo siempre te cantaré,
Canciones llenas de amor
Pero que todos recuerden
Que soy tu nieto Mayor

Yo soy la luz de tus ojos,
Y tu, eres la vida mía
Yo soy tus llantos, tus penas
Y tu, eres la vida mía.

Toma esta flor Abuelita,
Que te la manda Papito
Anque estén un poco tristes
Su perfume, está enterito.

Anibal Bourdon

Anibal Bourdon

Cosas de Loco

Todos me llaman poeta,
Porque sé de todo un poco
Tengo cosas de profeta,
y tengo cosas de loco.

Loco porque no he encontrado,
Una mujer que me quiera,
Y dejaré de ser loco
Cuando no sienta loqueras.

Loco porque tengo ansias,
De besarte, con locuras,
Y me beses locamente
Y hacer contigo diabluras.

Y si me dejas de amar,
En verdad me vuelvo loco
Y cuando suceda esto,
Es que me patina el coco.

Si el amor es una cosa,
Segun dicen los poetas,
Que empieza en el corazón
Y termina en la cabeza.

Anibal Bourdon

Mi Puerto Rico

No sé nada de cultura,
Ni de ciencias, ni de artes
Pero de mi Puerto Rico
Digo, que sí sé bastante.

Sé de los grandes poetas,
De grandes compositores
Como fue Don Rafael
Igual que Don Pedro Flores.

El Señor Albizu Campos
Tambien Luis Muñoz Marín
Yo se de el Grito de Lares
Cuando se formó el motín.

Sé de las grandes leyendas,
Que tiene mi Puerto Rico
Parece no tener nada
Pero es sabroso, bonito.

Si....yo les puedo cantar,
Y ahora, se lo contaré
Que a Puerto Rico Señores
Jamas yo lo negaré.

Y cuando sale la luna,
Las noches se ven mas bellas
Y las estrellas, brillantes
Siempre están al lado de ella.

Ruby M. Burns

Hope

Candles casting shadows
A robed figure holds a cross of gold,
A chapel resounds with voices in song.

A wise man reads the Torah,
A promise of the deliverance of his people.

The sun rises on the inscrutable face of
the Buddah, the faithful kneel.

Black hands clap to the rhythm of spirituals,
poignant with hope.

In a cathedral of trees a figure pauses
in communion with the Great Spirit
that this cup might pass and that humanity not
be destroyed from the face of the earth.

Time encircles the Mighty One.

Ana Cardona

there is a me

revealed only in anonymity

places unknown

with faces not to be seen

unveil me

unnerve me

know me not too well, my world

i vanish at the touch

Julio Perazza

Ana Cardona

perhaps in love

i have given myself
i have hidden myself
i have lost myself

José L. Garza

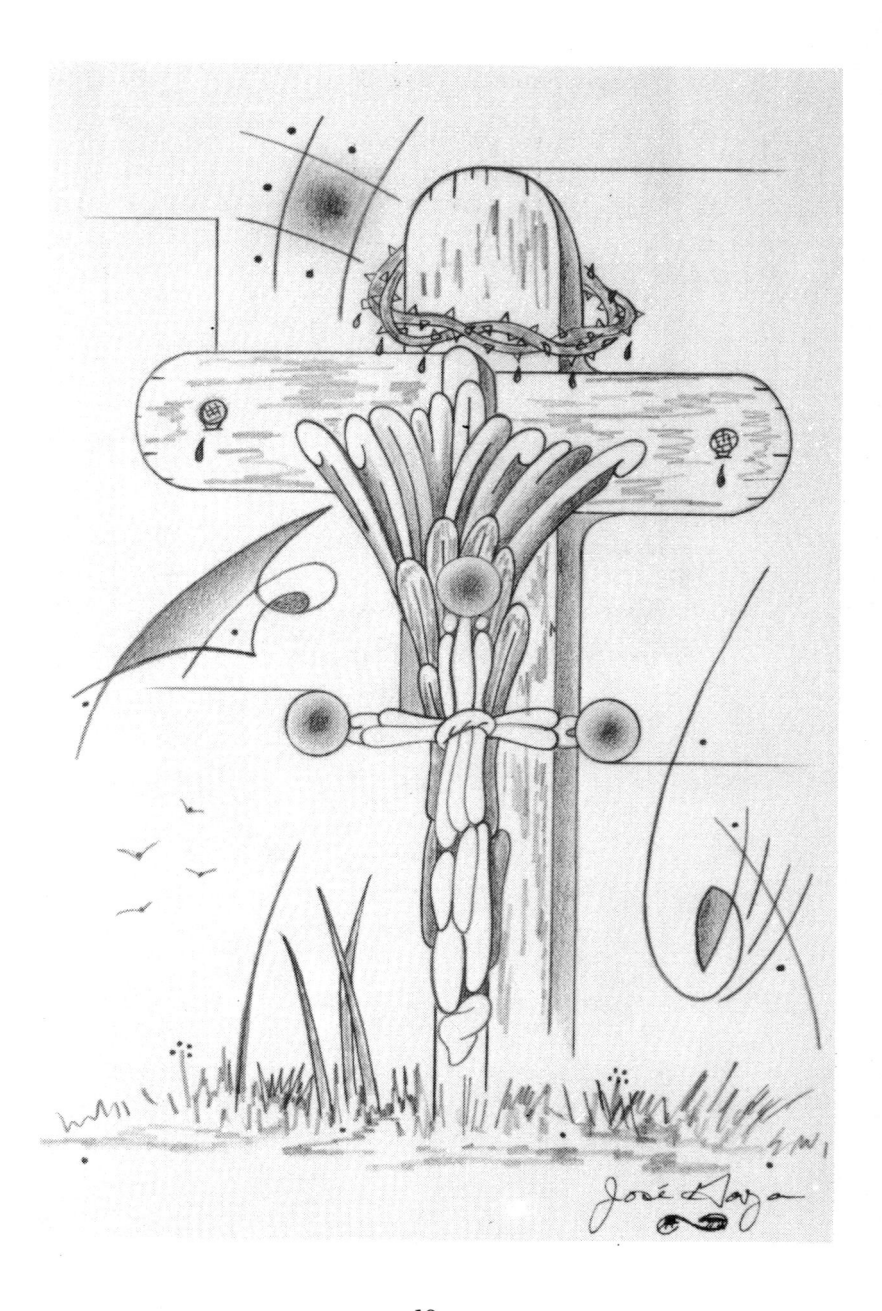

Ana Cardona

young boy of 14, son of man i know through
    generous happy sharing
shoots himself, is shot, by nickel-plated
    handgun

i am touched by the loss of a boy i know only
    in death

a community is brought close through this
    death-for-no-good-reason.

i loose myself in thought of the mothers, fathers,
    children, lovers,

feeling, losing, having stolen from them the
    presence,
the being, the life of their baby, their baby,
    their love,
their other, their self
the sobs and cries and

pain
the hollow loss
the mother's empty stare, carried, walked
down the aisle past her now dead baby son.

y padre, aguantando, apretando, gritando su dolor
en forma de nina de 4 anos
nina, imagen de nuestro amor.

amen.

Ana Luisa Barreto

Ana Cardona

```
        photographic evidence
                of
        deceptions twice denied

photographic tell-tale signs
      that what you said
           was hardly
             the truth
           and nothing
               but
            the truth
   so help me Kodachrome 25
```

Warren Augustus Hollier

Marcelle Douglas

The Villanelle of Conquest

Though they were met with outstretched hand
Their hate and ferocity inspired by greed and fear
They came to take away our land

Piece by piece they wrested the land
That they had traveled far and near
Though they were met with outstretched hand

They had no guile to match the man
Searching for a new frontier
They came to take away our land

There was no peace within the clan
Deprived we were of all that was dear
Though they were met with outstretched hand

To reservations and anonymity they did ban
Thus to our death and silent tear
They came to take away our land

They have weakened; it is time to plan
The future now for us is clear
Though they were met with outstretched hand
They came to take away our land

José L. Garza

Un Mensaje de Flatsville

Tierra Roja llamando como un imán
sube tu sonido como las nubes al viento
las nubes que dejan agua que transforma la rosa
su sangre colorada   colorada   y corriente
para bañar el terreno con semilla
para no olvidar
para obligar

                        para todos que caerón
                        inocentes desaparicidos
                        asesinados
                        todos ustedes sin país

fijense las chuparosas al orilla del monte grueso
vuela un compañero alegre junto con ellos
acaba de llegar el Argentino-Cubano-Boliviano
el comandante Ché   Boca Abierta
y sangrado colorado   colorado
de todo su pecho
llega preguntando –   que hemos hecho?

José L. Garza

Para Ti, Maria Luisa Torres P. de Sonora

              s t a r s h i n e
that ripples across the minds reflective edge
appearing   disappearing   to blend
into the warmed mist of a thousand distant dawns
compassionate window mirrors of the soul
smile and wonder at the marvel of it all

              e a r t h f i r e
magic-real   breathing   laughing sounds
nestled now in your silent waiting womb
in noiseless speech tell of the eons on eons
of the deepening wisdoms of the universe

              m o o n g l o w
rounded skylight slipping by   bright   then darker
peeking from behind air/water mountain valleys
that once floated our dream songs to one another
small   crisp   whispers
man woman voices here at this same place in time
joined together by a timeless embrace
                                      warm and safe

Hernán Castellano-Girón

Hernán Castellano-Girón

Cuando Pase Frente a la Casa Donde Nacio Aretha Franklin

Cuando pasé frente a la casa donde nació Aretha
   Franklin
Yo mismo había nacido hacía muchos meses
Había perdido la inocencia en el mismo vecindario

Pero esa tarde me llovió sobre mojado
Recuerdo que había ranas croando como en un sueño.

Mas allá, un crepúsculo ostentoso
De colores, formas, floraciones del cielo.
En el callejón, un vagabundo bebía
Una botella de Johnny Walker
Cubierta de un saquito de papel.
Los pastores negros predicaban a todo volumen
Desde una pequeña iglesia igual a todas las casas
Porque dios, en ese barrio, debe ser un milagro
   cotidiano.

De otro modo no sabría cómo manifestarse.

Ese dia toqué en el viejo piano de mis amigos Watson:
"Somewhere over the rainbow", como en 1968
Con Jorge Teillier y el chico Cardenas
-- Ambos poetas del sur, hijos de otro cielo --
Los tres más que bebidos, el día en que pasé
Frente a la casa en que nació y creció
   Aretha Franklin

Poco despues me tropecé con un gato muerto por la
   calle
Con un reloj de cristal, con una hembra madura
Calzando guantes de seda
Crucé las puertas de la aurora.

Hernán Castellano-Girón

Hernán Castellano-Girón

Lotus Blossom

La última vez que escuche a Duke Ellington
Tocaba "Lotus Blossom" en el Teatro-Circo
 "Caupolicán".
Me rodeaban putas y bandidos
Moscas y pulgas, y el humo de 10.000
Prohibidos cigarrillos. Microclima ecológico
O texto ilegible de una ciudad maldita. Un
 cigarro
De menos hubiese retardado el Golpe por diez anos.

Pero esto es nada más que el presente.
El entonces si era mágico: Duke se sentó al piano
Con su coleta de chino austral, como un radiante
 monstruo
Color calypso. Hizo callar a los bandidos y a las
 putas
Hizo detenerse a las pulgas y las moscas
En ese aire y ese tiempo fatal en todo, menos en
 eso.
Alli están todavía, ellos, ellas y nosotros
Fijos para siempre, desenfadados
Inauditos pájaros de un inmenso misterio

Marycruz Soto Gonzalez

encontré
una paloma que sola estaba,
y en sus ojos miré
tu imagen hermosa que con amor
siempre contemplé
      nunca
supe el motivo
de tu abandono por mi
pero quiero decirte
que siempre vivirás
dentro de mi.
      tu imagen
se perdió entre la lluvia
de sus ojos
y al quererte encontrar,
entre la lluvia, sin tu
imagen y perdido quedé.

Victoria González

Some Day

Some day
I'll raise my hand and voice
and ask questions I never
dared to ask before.
I'll make a fool of myself
on purpose.
I'll do things
in unconventional ways.
I'll tear down all my walls
(that took so long to build)
and destroy all barriers
in this world.
And the next day,
I'll slip back
into my unquestioning and
prejudiced self.

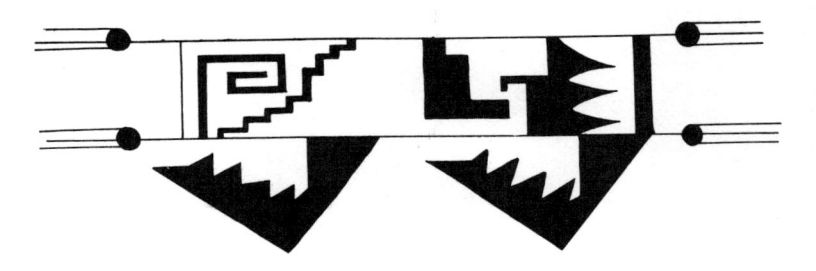

Victoria González

I Love the Way

```
    I love the way you think
       you're always right
          and then
don't take too long to admit it
      when you're wrong.
```

Lolita Hernandez-Gray

Early Morning

The fingers of my mind reach out
and grab the panic
an empty something
weighing on my every breath
and choking the knotted dreams in my stomach.

It was nice in the days of a shallow but flowing youth.
Manageable loneliness
and measurable tears
that would evaporate with the arrival of
the promises promised.

There was plenty of time to explore
and plenty of time
to ease away from reality
just a bit.

Time to tolerate pain
as a wrinkle in the laughter of discovery.
Everything always new – really new...
and great.

Time to smile fully
to welcome the next bout with the next answer
and Hoodoo Blues
that somehow got danced away.

Time to misjudge
knowing that time itself would teach the scars.

Loneliness was a toy top to spin
and then stop.

There's no stopping now –
the spin speeds
and bits of painted memories fly off
exposing new memories

for which there is no time

William Mora, Jr.

Lolita Hernandez-Gray

To an Old West Indian Woman

who must daily live her defeat
dressed in her raggedness:
her hair with its undyeable roots,
ill fitting false teeth, claws for toenails...
and her subtle funk –
a first stage of death
which she must welcome
as realer than anything –
anything that her distant TV friends can offer.

So she dreams dreams.
Everydayanewdream...
off to Miami
off to Hot Springs
off to Puerto Rico
off to Australia
off to any substitute warmth
for her Trinidad warmth.

But somehow
behind her dull eyes
she remembers seeing
all that she has seen
to make her laugh
still
yesterday's laughter
and sometimes forget
today's everyday
pain.

When she can't forget
she lifts up her dress
shamelessly exposing
an   oldwomanhood
ulcerated

and hurting...

Warren Augustus Hollier

"Ascension of Night"

Warren Augustus Hollier

Ascension of Night

She moves like a whisper
Uncovering the shadows that
Have been hidden by day

Slowly and silently pushing
All light out of her path;
Forcing her cooling grip
To enfold and drain the
Warmth from everything
She touches.

Her dark hair sweeping
Through the tall grass and
Combing the branches of the
Trees, stills the air and
Lays a hush upon the land.

She is gentle and will
let you dream until her
Sister returns for she
Is the night.

William Mora, Jr.

Fred Mora

The Adult

They walk, talk, some think.
They laugh, cry, mostly when they drink.

They steal, cheat, only for more gold.
They're mean, selfish, just to be bold.

They give, but only to receive.
Only for themselves to achieve.

They commit adultery then lie.
Thinking they're really sly.

I don't want to be one of these adults.
I don't want to have these undesirable faults.

I want to offer, follow, praise.
I want to help bring this world out of this craze.

I want to love these adults.
Help them out with their faults.

I want to be a man.
But most of all remain a child in Christ's hand.

William Mora, Jr.

William Mora, Jr.

Moon Struck

The year 3000, the month Venus, date the 50th, the time 20:00 and one hundred minutes, a new computerized man is born. His name – Neal Floyd, which has been planted since 1961 in the air of existence; finally grown and hatched out of its silver egg shell. His permission rights were read to him, then he was given a room with four sides of glass. Neal was left alone for a test. Finally, I made it to the mechanized world in the Universe. Here I am sitting in my glass room with thousands of buttons to choose from and a screen to watch the entire universe at work – what a dramatic systematized creation of existence.

Anyway, I pressed the button moonstruck. I knew I had committed a crime without permission rights. I still proceeded with the project.

The moon had risen out of the deep orange sea, the moon was bright purple. I had stared for about 3 seconds, then the lunar module approached with the moonstruck tape. The waves struck my brain, it felt like a multi-needles injected to my brain. The brain was wide open. The process was slow. Somehow the lunatic worms snuck in before the tape was in. The worms didn't have permission to enter. The worms told me that I also didn't have permission to proceed with the project of moonstruck. I said, "right", they laughed and said, "Guess what? The tape is in session, Floyd, and you are now a lunatic – a computerized man – now we are 1000% behind you, sir!"

William Mora, Jr.

William Mora, Jr.

Behind Time

    You there – Do you believe in time?
Well forget it! I'll tell you why. I am here,
and you are here, but yet we're still behind time.
We'll never catch the right time.
The only time you have is to live and die.

    You there – time has been here before
your time, and it stays here, not you or me.

    You there – you are the one that dies
not time.

    You there – time keeps going rolling forever,
not the living, you understand,
you timeless clock, trying to keep yourself
in order, forget it.

    You there – Don't matter now, you are
still behind time.

    You there – are you still here

    You there – where are you

    You there – Do you exist

    You there – There's no world

    You there – have your rights of
                Mental

    You there – remember this!
        time for school
        time to eat
        time for work
        time to live and a time to die

    Don't you see, since you were born
its been the same time for everything
important, nothing for your self,
No matter what you think, you're
still behind time.

    Where are you now!

Delfin Muñoz

The Shade of Steam Heat

We travel from day
to night
Yet the shadows
all surround us
We ask for the ham
We ask for the cheese
but mondongo is on
our breath
We ask for disco
We ask for the rock
but listen to Willie y Celia
The shadows
continue from day to night
We walk quite proudly
then shout quite loudly,
"Que pasa, mamita?"
We dress quite prissly
but dance one only
to a salsa in the wind
And it is the shadows
of the night and day
the shade of steam heat
that are the good part
the very best part

Delfin Muñoz

If It Were

If it were a choice of songs
I would belong
If it were a right or wrong
I would belong
But since it is a
choice of color
I don't believe
I ever will belong

It's not wear these clothes
and don't forget what to say
It's your skin keeps you
from the American way

Lana Douglas

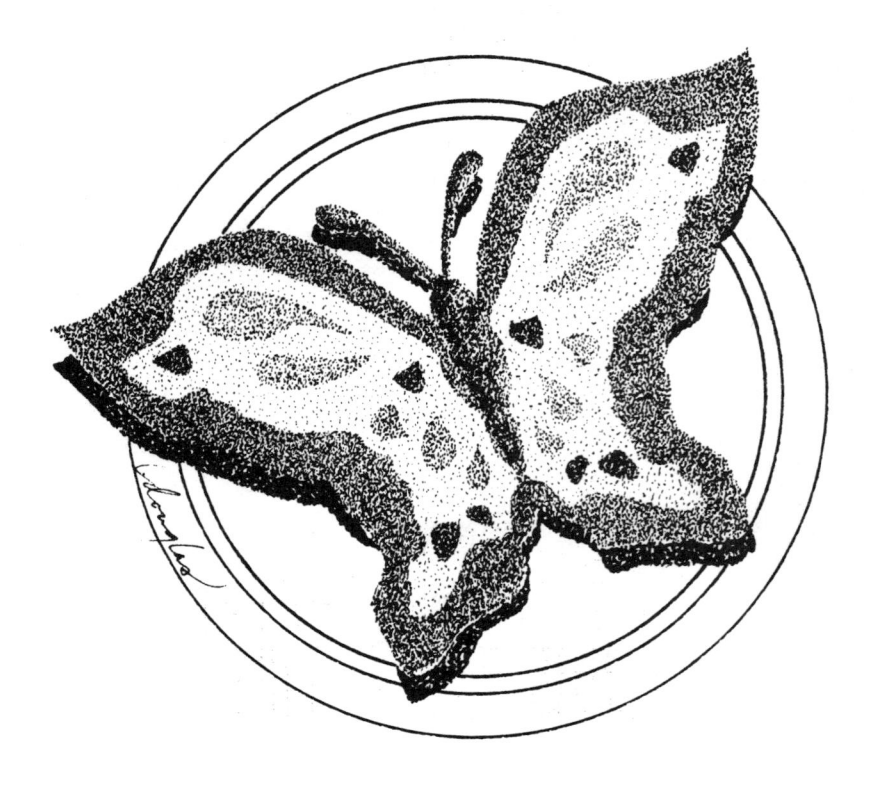

Delfin Muñoz

Mystery and Shadow

I am a glimpse of the unseen that all see
I am the shadow of doubt and mystery
Where lurks
the hopeless
in darkness and despair
the triumphant
with
their pleasure and their flair
and those
with no identity
who from
no glass can truly see
who for no past
can truly feel
who beg for
a name while they kneel
but the triumphant
ride through
as if with no tomorrow
and the others
the others
in misery and sorrow
neither lead nor follow
but in their waste lay low

Delfin Muñoz

Centuries of Slavery

After centuries of slavery,
it was put to me:
"Where are your manners?"
"Your central policy planners?"
"Don't you want to get ahead?"
"Don't you want your children fed?"
As I struggled from my chains
I would hear these foul refrains:
"You live in filth and poverty,
which is where you ought to be."
"You haven't the dignity to rise from the street.
Nor the culture from which the wise and strong compete."
And when I broke my chains and gathered freedom to me,
I was told life would not be easy for dogs, swine, and me.
And lo, the prophecy is true,
I've not yet a free man's due.

Rosa Maria Muñoz

Con los ojos del alma
veo, como se destruye
esta Humanidad, y al pasar
por la máquina del tiempo,
en cada capítulo de mi alma,
se abren las puertas de
egoísmo, maldad y vanidad
que hay en esta podrida
      sociedad
y en cada ventana de mi alma,
sale el fuego de una criatura
celestial que con sus fibras
candentes y amorosas, exploran
las lagunas obscuras de mi tiempo.
Y esa luz divina traspasa las fibras
de estas criaturas celestial,
llenándolas de claridad a esta
corrupta y podrida sociedad.

Rosa Maria Muñoz

Padre Nuestro, que estás
en algun lugar del Universo
Santificados sean aquellos
que no tienen de comer

Líbranos del tirano, imperialista
      y opresor
Perdónanos nuestras deudas y
haz que el imperialista perdone
a sus embrollones, y a todos
      sus deudores.
No nos dejes caer en las garras
del opresor, más líbranos de todo
mal como la guerra nuclear.

Rosa Maria Muñoz

Man greatest evil on earth
crawling like a serpent at night
tearing humanities innocent heart
man trying to reach the door of
knowledge through the path of disgrace
Tearing the limbs of a heavenly creature
blaspheming the masterpiece of all times
ruling on the develish, like a ball of fire
Man crying his shame to the heavenly
machinery that only makes time,
which has the numbness of a beggar
crawling at night for the bread of light
Man cry your disgrace, to the creature
        of darkness
which only crawls on hate
       but not faith.

José L. Garza

Nemene

Two Colors

Issues are black or white
red or brown is not right
suppose we mix black and white
would a gray color be all-right?
this Indian sits at the philosophy class
the issue the constitution due process
skip the greed for land and grass
that turned the white man into an ass
one hundred and nine days of rye profusion
great deficits and oppressive pollution
my land was virgin and my people free
before smith and jones went on a spree
deceiving and cheating advanced to a degree
but to make it legal concoted a decree
no more treaties or crystal beads
the proud Indian has no bed
culture and children being raped
to a black and white society he looks sad
two colors they would say
forget the Indian he is RED.

Ana Luisa Barreto

Nemene

This Clay

They call it democracy
I call it bureaucracy
the process of enslaving
a human being to a simple number
not even a deviated primate
just a simple number
reducing a person to a number
and the expected   conditioned response
the concept
the principle brought to America
by God fearing puritans
the concept of a melting pot
everybody everything
mixed together
like sand shale limestone
to form a new type of cement
a new flexible clay
to mold whichever way

I AM to prove that this clay
MY CLAY
does not assimilate
to no abstract freedom
freedom of speech
freedom of religion
freedom of individual?
I AM going to pound on this clay
with MY fists
to form with MY   hands
a true image
MY own image.

Ana Luisa Barreto

Patti Orozco

23rd Street-Detroit

<u>grandpa Manuels house</u>

that smell
of grandpa's house
on 23rd
of tortillas
frying
albondigas
greasy soup
beans and rice
make a little taco

sweet Mexican candy
sipping coffee
out of his saucer
while he talked
to himself
about the revolution.

how I loved those days

<u>grandma Botellos house</u>

white picket fence
three little bears
on the hill
where we use to play
and the trees
that would touch the sky
where dreams would come true

chipped paint
old wood
broken ear
Ambassador Bridge
and tall weeds
where houses once stood.

where my dreams are fulfilled

Patti Orozco

like a rat
slips through the door
up the steps
runs down the ramp to my third door
noise of the freeway
the window my pillow
i'm home
and then the day
i start to think
and my grandmother is yelling
to come down and eat chop suey
i don't know
maybe a little—
but i'm thinking of the funeral home
this morning
and she doesn't understand
so i eat chop suey

poor antonio
poor antonio

i stood there with my mother
poor antonio, she said
we stood there us two
silent

poor antonio

in a suit
in a grey felt casket
(the American dream)
two bouquets of flowers
one to each side
above his head lay a crucifix
of baby pink roses from his daughter

more....

Patti Orozco

i'm gonna get straight he'd say
i'm gonna get straight
when my daughter comes to Detroit
i'm gonna get straight

we stood there
us two
silent

the door broke open
kids
they stood at the very back
afraid to approach

outside was hot
humid
back at work
the free lunches had just arrived
sworms of kids tearing down the hallway
i knew many of them
dirty little feet

in moms office there was a man
away from these parts for a long time
on junk
sincere
he blamed the city

waiting in the hall there was a girl
on glue
pregnant

outside it was hot
antonio was everywhere
dirt kicked up in little cyclones
from passing trucks
hitting me in the eyes
new cadillacs   more....

Patti Orozco

```
like a rat
slips through the door
up the steps
runs down the ramp
to my third door
noise of the freeway
the window   my pillow
i'm home
```

José L. Garza

Rachel Perazza

A Writer Finds Himself

A writer finds himself
through his words.
Through his ever-changing
Life,
along with the emotions too.
Through his ever-widening look
of his world,
and all that goes on within it.

A writer, constantly writing,
A writer, constantly telling
of his life,
finding his way through his poems.
Finding his life and its answers
through his words,
and free-flowing that which is
unattainably free-flowing
in his life.

A writer feels too much,
A writer knows too much,
and sometimes would rather
just keep it all
to himself,
and not write
at all.

Abel Piñeiro

Looking for Other Places

I remember a crazy brother, a dreamy sister
an angry father, a helpless mother,
and more sisters, selfish and bossy
more brothers....wreckless, naive
and another...(in the basement, meditating)
looking for something called "inner peace"
It wasn't me...

I was wandering among the railroad tracks
at the river's edge
among empty warehouses and torn factories,
among charcoal piles and heaps of tires...
whittling sticks into spears with my little
      pirate's knife
pretending I might have to fight for my life
scouting all over this mystical place
digging for old bones, old bottles
for pennies and old indian-head nickels,
and finding none without a faded face....

I didn't know what "peace" was
I just wanted QUIET...for a moment,
to hear my heart beat
FREEDOM......forever
to move about unshackled to a yard, a house,
a room, a clock...
to be alone....
to talk to myself and ponder things without
      interruption
and I'd climb up on a wall towering high above
      the ground
and watch the sacred place like a soldier or a
king and gazing down from my throne
it had a splendor all its own:
when the sun would command with its blazing might,
"Grey wall, grey slabs, grey all turn to white!"

Abel Piñeiro

and out from their cracks
the dry weed and dry grass would glisten like gold,
brilliant yellow strings of brass.

The dark, murky river would turn silver and shine
like it does in a poem
broken windows and fragments of glass would sparkle
like diamonds embedded in stone....

Then in these moments of happiness and wonderment,
my misery would become so clear to me...by its
    absence.

The sun would go, eventually, and it woud be
    getting late.
I'd get hungry, and I'd hate to be around when it
    got dark.
So out on to the streets, across the empty lots,
and through the park....HOME
and at night, in bed, my mind would wander by way of
    factory land
where the faint echoes of a pounding drum, the soft,
moaning, mechanical hum...would lull me to sleep,
looking for other places I'd rather be.

Carolina Ramon

Circles of color
Floating, swimming in the air
Brightly shining like the
    midnight light
Sparkling, twinkling, dusting
    all around
Moving like the moons of Jupiter
going where you are
Seeing only circles of color
Warms

José L. Garza

Marc Sanchez

Abuela

In my grandmother's mind there were images of
swirling dust rising from
the Indian earth against the sun torn mountain
ceiling and wet trees
rooted in deep white fields through a clear
night's drift.
Blurred images from diffuse memory painful
and confused of narrow
streets and swollen children unable to escape
the howl of hunger.
Images flashing vivid without explanations
images dark and quick that never were seen
images unborn lost in the voids
images of me.

Lana Douglas

Marc Sanchez

Estella at 29

To wake awash in the light of the fleeing sun
and not feel the ache of a death pulling earth,
she drank herself to depthless swoons in closing
time bars where the only message she received was
last call
Her tender eyelids almost closed she spoke of our
native land and the eternity of pain
She lost herself in the breathing sweating flesh
of men clawing for morning through the worst of
nights
She listened to Rolando S. who filled body bags
in nam at seventeen and returned to sit on the
same barstool for three years and stared at god
knows what sights in the darkening mirror.
Estella of the stars wounded in her beauty.
There is no universe glittering with a thousand
lights to guide her home,
so tonight she walks alone in darkness with iron
colored drizzle afraid only of turning thirty.

Jacqueline Sanchez

Inner City Children

Running wild in the streets
asking for attention,
yearning for affection,
aiming for realistic dreams,
needing security,
satisfaction;
hundreds of children
either orphaned or homeless,
pushed from the nest needlessly.
Empty lives out on the street,
searching.

Jacqueline Sanchez

Goddess of Morning Dew

Goddess of early morning sun
bless this earth,
body of my soul;
bless the trees,
branches of my inner thoughts;
bless the fruits thereof,
fruits of my womb;
bless the birds of flight,
the heart beat of my being.

Goddess of early morning sun,
bless the early morning dew
that caresses my every fiber
so as to nourish my existence,
which is a viable extension
of your existence

Goddess of early morning dew
hear my plea.

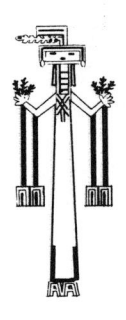

William Mora, Jr.

Trinidad Sánchez, S.J., Hno.

Martyrs by Mistake en Centro America

In memory of Arthur Fusco 3/3/85

Arthur Fusco, 22 years old
a handsome man – "the most striking thing is his
smile – it is as wide as his face!"
"He was very much like an enthusiastic large little
      boy ....
when you met him he made you feel good, exuberance,
      energy."
"He had many friends."

La mama, his only mother, called him
"my masterpiece" – her very best!
Her BOY BLUE had become her PIETA.

Fluent in Spanish, he acted as interpreter
for those que no hablaban español
en Braus Laguna, Honduras.

The Pentagon called it "Civic Action!"
"FIRE IN THE HOLE IN 5 MINUTES ....
 FIRE IN THE HOLE IN 4 MINUTES ....
 FIRE IN THE HOLE IN 2 MINUTES ....
 FIRE IN THE HOLE!"

There was no radio
no way of hearing the warning over the noise
of a 35 horsepower motor.
There were no buoys marking the demolition site.

Falling down in bits and pieces.
Did Fusco think it might have been better for him
to have given his life para su gente de Nueva York!

Las noticias, the news – is not clear
no way of confirming it was his body!
Did Mike Uyeda, the Japanese American, his
companion recall the memorias of his ancestors
memories of Hiroshima!

Trinidad Sánchez, S.J., Hno.

Martyrs by mistake....
maybe it was a mistake...
that they entered the navy-
that they did not refuse to go to Centro America.

Mistake or not
ustedes saben bien
igual que yo
que ellos eran
victimas
del intervencion injusta
del gobierno gringo
en Centro America!

Mistake or not
you know fully well
that they were
victims
of the unjust intervention
of the gringo government
in Centro America!

José L. Garza

Trinidad Sánchez, S.J., Hno.

Monseñor Oscar Romero–Presente

"Monseñor Romero!"
"PRESENTE!"
"Por cierto se presentó
con los pobres / los marjinados
a traerles la buena nueva.

Por cierto se presentó
con los mas pequeños
a conocer a escuchar
a compartir su vida.

"Monseñor Romero!"
"PRESENTE!"
Por cierto se presentó
se encarnó en el sufrimiento
de su pueblo Salvadoreño.

Por cierto se presentó
como mensajero del Senor
a denunciar las injusticias
de la intervención
del gobierno gringo.

"Monseñor Romero!"
"PRESENTE!"
Por cierto se presentó
como amenaza a los multinacionales,
a los militares / a los ricos.

Por cierto se presentó
como fiel cristiano
persona de fe
comprometido a la justicia.

Trinidad Sánchez, S.J., Hno.

"Monseñor Romero!"
"PRESENTE!"
Por cierto se presentó
a llamarnos a nosotros
como compañeros
de hacer lo mismo.

Por cierto
agradecemos tu vida
aquí con nosotros
ayer / hoy / y para siempre!

"Monseñor Romero!"
"PRESENTE!"
"PRESENTE!"
"PRESENTE!"

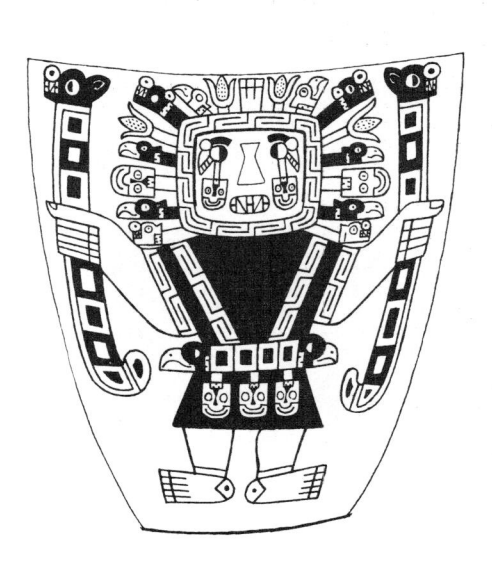

BIOGRAPHICAL NOTES

Barreto, Ana Luisa : Was born in Acapulco, Guerrero, Mexico. She was involved with the historical mural painted at the Government Building in Acapulco, Guerrero and has had several art exhibitions in that same city.
In 1976 she moved to Mexico City to study at The National School of Fine Arts where she completed her Bachelor of Visual Arts Degree. She has supervised the production of and created many posters, brochures, flyers and silkscreens for a Rape Crisis Center in Mexico City. She has established herself as an illustrator in the Mexican magazines "Fem" and "El Afiliado".

Bourdon, Anibal : Was born in the town of Moca, Puerto Rico. He is a singer/composer with the group "Conjunto Sabor". Anibal comes from a loving large family of 15 and many are also singers or poets. He is married and has three children.

Burns, Ruby Mae : Was born at Indian Mound, Tennessee in 1907. She is of Cherokee and German descent and worked as a sharecropper in the tobacco fields as a child. Ruby is the mother of two daughters.

Cardona, Ana : Bronx born.
Manhattan grown.
Puerto Rican, Michigan muse.
Mouthpiece for the age-old silenced voices.
Moon child.
Twin soul.
On the way.
Just passing through.

Douglas, M. Lana : Creek Indian born and raised in Detroit. She is an art teacher with the Detroit Public School System and is currently assigned to the Children's Museum. Lana is a free lance artist, illustrator, graphic design artist and a calligrapher. Other interests include ballet and tennis.

Douglas, Marcelle : Creek Indian born in Oklahoma and a Michigan resident for over 34 years. She is a teacher with Headstart, a part time student at Wayne State University majoring in English and a mother of six children, grandmother with six grandchildren. Her interests are playing piano, knitting, crocheting, sewing, reading and travel.

Garza, José Leyva : Was born in San Antonio, Texas and raised in Detroit. He was a news and feature writer for Conciencia Libre and The South End newspapers (1971-1974). His artwork was published in Song For Maya (1983). His poetry and short stories have appeared in a number of publications including the American Indian art journal Akwekon (1985), the anthology Nostalgia for the Present (1985), The Great Lakes Review (1985) and The Native Sun (1985). Other interests include counting the bullet holes in the Alamo.

Girón, Hernán Castellano- : Is an artist/poet born in 1937. He studied and taught at The University of Chile at Santiago and is currently in exile. He lived in Italy from 1974-1981. He lives in Detroit and is a doctoral fellow at Wayne State University.

González, Marycruz Soto : Was born in Detroit in 1968. She lived and studied in Monterrey, Nuevo Leon, Mexico for 16 years. She started writing at the age of 12 and is currently a student in Detroit at Holy Redeemer High School.

Gonzalez, Victoria : Was born in 1969 in Santiago, Chile. Her parents are from Nicaragua and the United States. She has lived in Matagalpa, Nicaragua for 13 years and has been living in the United States since 1983. Victoria has lived one year in Detroit and is currently a student at Holy Redeemer High School. Her father still lives in Nicaragua and she plans to visit there next summer.

Gray, Lolita Hernandez : Started writing poetry in 1971 while working with various inner city theatre groups. Both of her parents are West Indian. Her mother was a great storyteller and taught Lolita how to read from poetry books. Lolita says, "It is to her that I owe my strivings to write poetry."

Hollier, Warren Augustus : Creek Indian born in California and a Michigan resident for 33 years. He has a Masters Degree in Education and is an art teacher for the Detroit Public School System. He was named the "Teacher of the Year at Mumford High School - 1985". Warren is a metalsmith, ceramic designer, illustrator, graphic designer, and technical illustrator. Other interests include automotive sports and writing.

Mora, Fred : Is a poet and a photographer.

Mora, William Jr. : Was born in Urbana, Ohio in 1961. He is an artist and a musician. William did alot of traveling as part of the migrant labor force in the midwestern United States. In 1973 the family moved to Detroit where they have lived since. He has exhibited his artwork in 22 exhibits in the Detroit area and painted two wall murals in the community of southwest Detroit. William is a contemporary artist who works in the experimental world of "surrealism, abstractism, muralism, idealism, and imaginalism with objects that follow the Moraism Movement Originalistic".

Muñoz, Delfin : Is a Performing Arts' graduate from Cass Technical High School and has recieved a B.A. in Mass Communications from Wayne State University. He is working on his first novel, tentatively titled "My Life Among the Iguanas".

Muñoz, Rosa Maria : Began writing poetry at a writing workshop at the University of Puerto Rico. Two poems will be published soon in The New Voices of American Poetry. She is currently a student at Wayne State University.

Nemene (José M. Moreno) : Is a mestizo-Comanche born in the "magico Valle del Rio Grande", Texas. He is 36 years of age and has been a migrant worker for a majority of his life. He is self educated until he started his adult education at SPSM (Jackson Prison) and is currently in his third year of college. His goal is to major in Sociology. His vocations are to sing, paint and write, write, and write.

Orozco, Patti : I have spent my life documenting it
I grew up here - an artist/writer/painter
loving it - hating it
looking - wondering - seeing nothing
confronted with everything
wanting to leave- adoringly attached

It is more than a subculture
it is on the edge
balanced by tradition
disturbed by the new
sustained by the old
revisited - humorous

I take from the industrial sounds
like a hummingbird of its mysterious
peaceful, haunting dawn

Perazza, Julio : Has been making art for 34 years. He received his B.F.A. and M.F.A. in Fine Arts. He recently recieved the Juried Best Show Award at the Michigan Hispanic Exhibition 1985.

Perazza, Rachel : Was born in Detroit 29 years ago and has lived in the downriver area for the last 17 years. She is attending Henry Ford Community College and hopes to teach emotionally disturbed or gifted children. She is currently employed as a Domestic Engineer. Rachel has been writing poems and short stories over the last 3 years. She enjoys dancing, drawing, metaphysics and doing astrological readings.

Piñeiro, Abel : Was born in Detroit in 1965, the last in a family of nine. He states that he is "a college 'walk-out' (I never dropped out of anything), who could cut it, but had a dull knife. Dulled with a shortage of finances, a need to work full time and a general restlessness as has been known to afflict us young people". He is skilled in working with children and his passion is in music and writing. In the future hopes for marriage and growth with Cathy. His love is for God and all things considered.

Ramon, Carolina : Is an artist and writer.

Sanchez, Jacqueline R. : Was, is and will always be a Vigorian Poet. Born in 1946, she is editor-publisher of The Sounds of Poetry and founder-president of The Latino Poets Association. She has been published in various anthologies and periodicals across the U.S.A. since 1975. Author of three chapbooks: Gypsy Melody in the Mist of the Sea, Running Free and More ... and Mine Eyes Have Seen. She is a member of The Poetry Society of Michigan and has been listed in the American Writers of The Bi-Centennial Era (1976), Who's Who in Poetry (1978), Directory of Active Michigan Poets (1983) and the Directory of Michigan Literary Publishers (1984).

Sanchez, Marc : His short stories have appeared in Nuestro, El Grito Del Sol, and The New York Review. Another will appear in an upcoming issue of The Bilingual Review. His poetry was published in The Wayne Review. Marc won the Tompkins Literary Award from Wayne State University in 1980.

Sánchez, Trinidad - S.J., Hno. : Is the author of two Books of Poems by Father & Son, Volumes I and II. His poems have been published in various other publications and has done readings in San Antonio, Toledo, Lansing, Ypsilanti, Port Huron, Battle Creek and Detroit. In Detroit he is active with Casa de Unidad and Horizons in Poetry.